I0820280

HOW FAST CAN I RUN?

BLACK RABBIT BOOKS

Black Rabbit Books
P.O. Box 227
Mankato, MN 56001
www.blackrabbitbooks.com

Library edition published in 2026 by Black Rabbit Books.
This library-bound edition is reprinted by arrangement with Rebel Girls, Inc.

Text by Calliope Glass and Jess Harriton | Illustrations by Saoirse Lou
Art direction and design by Giulia Flamini | Cover design by Kristen Brittain

Cataloging-in-Publication Data is available at the Library of Congress.
ISBN 978-1-64582-574-6

Printed in China

HOW FAST CAN I RUN?

Tales of Extraordinary Women

Written by Calliope Glass
and Jess Harriton
Illustrated by Saoirse Lou

Once there were seven brave women who had big questions.

Will I defy the odds?

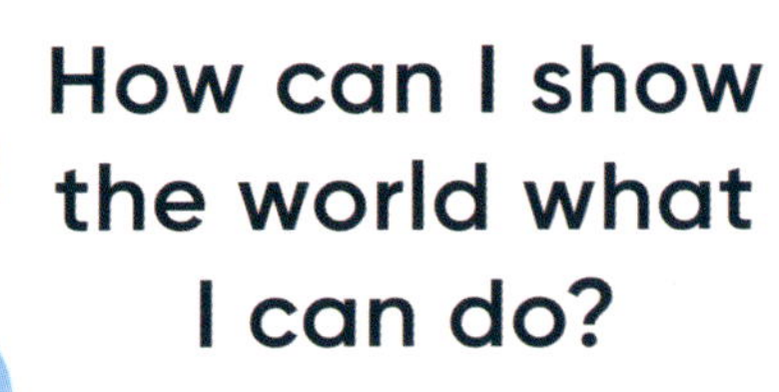

Their questions needed answers, so off they went to find them.

"How fast can I run?"
asked Elaine.

JAMAICA

"How many times can I flip?"
asked Simone.

"How much can I lift?"
asked Hidilyn.

"How far can I sail?"
asked Laura.

"How many goals can I score?" asked Marta.

"How high can I soar?"
asked Chloe.

#1

"How do I find
my favorite sport?"
asked Tegan.

To find their answers, they trained and practiced and challenged themselves. Sometimes they won, and sometimes they lost, but they never gave up.

Soon it will be your turn. What questions will you ask? How will you find your answers? With your courage and determination, you will make your mark too.

ELAINE THOMPSON-HERAH
Jamaican sprinter Elaine Thompson-Herah is famous for her lightning speed. She discovered her love of running as a child, but it wasn't until she was in college that she started seriously chasing her Olympic dream. Since then, Elaine has won five Olympic gold medals and set multiple records. She is one of the fastest women alive!

TEGAN VINCENT-COOKE
Tegan Vincent-Cooke is a para dressage rider from the United Kingdom. Tegan was born with cerebral palsy, which makes it hard for her to move her muscles. The first time Tegan tried horseback riding she felt her body relax. She knew dressage was the sport for her. Tegan has competed throughout the UK and looks forward to competing in the Paralympics.

HIDILYN DIAZ
Hidilyn Diaz discovered she was strong when she had to carry jugs of water from the well to her family's house. She practiced lifting with metal hubcaps and cement blocks. When she was 17, she joined the national weightlifting team. Hidilyn competed in three Olympics without winning any medals. She kept training and, in 2021, she made history by becoming the first person from the Philippines to win gold.

CHLOE KIM

Chloe Kim fell in love with snowboarding when she was just four years old. Chloe trained at home in California and in the majestic Swiss Alps. She went on to compete in the X Games and the Olympics. In the 2018 Olympics, she won gold and became the first woman to land two consecutive 1080s—that's a trick where the snowboarder spins three times high in the air! In 2022, Chloe won another gold medal, making her the first woman ever to win two gold medals on the halfpipe.

MARTA VIEIRA DA SILVA

As a little girl in Brazil, Marta Vieira da Silva didn't know many other girls who were drawn to soccer. But that didn't stop her. She honed her skills with the neighborhood boys and later took her talents all over the world. Marta has played in five World Cups and scored more goals than any other player. She's also scored more international goals than any Brazilian player, male or female. No wonder Marta is known as the Queen of Soccer!

LAURA DEKKER

Dutch sailor Laura Dekker is the youngest person to circumnavigate the globe solo. From the time she was a little girl, Laura dreamed of going on a big sailing trip all by herself, and when she was just 16 years old, she got her wish. On her trip around the world, Laura navigated through storms and rough seas. She got to explore the volcanic island of Bora Bora and marvel at giant sea turtles in the Galapagos.

SIMONE BILES

American gymnast Simone Biles discovered gymnastics on a school field trip. Now a four-time gold medalist, Simone is considered one of the greatest gymnasts of all time. Off the mat, Simone has spoken out about the importance of mental health. Her talent and honesty make her an inspiration to young athletes everywhere.

JAMAICA